JAPANESE HOKKUS

BY

YONE NOGUCHI

BOSTON
1920

PUBLIC DOMAIN POETS

Editor: Dick Whyte   —: No.V :—   May 2022

-->≥⁄≤⊱-

YONEJIRŌ NOGUCHI **(1875–1947)** was born in Tsushima, and went to Keiō University, in Tōkyō. At age **18** he moved to San Francisco, and soon after decided to become a poet. While English poetry in the 1800s was typically defined by its use of metered rhythm and rhyme, Noguchi wrote unrhymed verse in 'free' rhythms, taking inspiration from Japanese forms like tanka and hokku, and the poems of Walt Whitman, one of the only widely known English-language 'free verse' poets at the time. Noguchi is the earliest known writer of English-language haiku (then called hokku), and one of the earliest English-language poets to work exclusively in 'free verse', after Whitman. Between 1896-1920 Noguchi published 7 collections of English verse, several articles on hokku, and 2 widely read books of essays on the relationship between Japanese and Western poetics; and his work would go on to influence numerous significant poets of the post-1913 'new verse' movements, including Adelaide Crapsey, Amy Lowell, Ezra Pound, John Gould Fletcher, Lewis Alexander, E.E. Cummings (et al.).

-->≥⁄≤⊱-

'Hokku': Selected from *Japanese Hokkus* (The Four Seas Co., 1920); previously published *The Egoist* (Nov. 1916), & *Poetry* (Nov. 1919), etc. 'Early Hokku': from 'Shisen Miraa to Sankyo no Nikki' ['Diary of Mountain Life with the Great Poet Miller', 1897] (*Eibun Shinshi*, March 1904); '[street]' (1902); '[leaves]', '[light]', '[flowers]', '[love]', '[speak]', & '[waking]' ('Hokku', *Teikoku Bungaku*, 1903; 'A Proposal to American Poets', *The Reader*, 1904, etc.). 'Selected Poems': [1] *Seen & Unseen* (Burgess & Garnett, 1896); [2-6] 'Shisen Miraa...' (1897); [7] *The Voice of the Valley* (Doxey Press, 1897); [8-16] *From the Eastern Sea* (At the Unicorn, 1903); [10] with Florence Lundborg (*The Lark*, April 1897); [17] *Japan of Sword & Love* (Kanao Bunyendo, 1905); [18-20] *The Summer Cloud* (The Shunyodo, 1906); and [21-33] *The Pilgrimage* (The Valley Press, 1909). 'Notes on Hokku': Excerpts from 'A Japanese on English Poetry' (*The Academy*, Feb. 1912), 'Hokku' (*The Academy*, July 1912), 'What Is A Hokku Poem?' (*Rhythm*, Jan. 1913), and Noguchi's two books of essays, *Through the Torii* (The Four Seas Co., 1914), and *The Spirit of Japanese Poetry* (E.P. Dutton & Co., 1914).

Cover: William Keith – 'Dreams I & II' (*The Lark*, Nov. 1896). Inside: Florence Lundborg – 'Bird' (Nov. 1896); E.C. Peixotto – 'The Lark Soars' (*The Epilark*, May 1897); Ogata Kōrin – 'Trees', 'Rooster', 'Flowers', & 'Fan', in Noguchi's *Kōrin* (Elkin Mathews, 1922); M. Takahashi – 'Sketch'; & 'At Home' (*The Overland Monthly*, Jan. 1900); 'At Work' (*The Bookman*, Dec. 1900); 'In Tōkyō' (*National Magazine*, April 1906); O Yeto – 'Portrait' (Oct. 1901); Charles W. Hearn – 'Photo Portrait I' (1903); Langdon Coburn – 'Photo Portrait II' (1913); Yoshio Markino – 'Portrait', in *The Story of Yone Noguchi: Told By Himself* (Chatto & Windus, 1914), etc.

PUBLIC DOMAIN PRESS
Aotearoa / New Zealand

ISBN: 978-0-473-63085-0 (print) • 978-0-473-63086-7 (kindle)
978-0-473-63087-4 (pdf)

YONE NOGUCHI

JAPANESE HOKKU & OTHER VERSES

~~~~~~~~~~~~~~~~~~~~~~~~~~~~~~~~~~~~

JAPANESE HOKKU

A selection of hokku & tanka-influenced
verse in English, published 1920.

EARLY HOKKU

A selection of Noguchi's earliest hokku in English,
written & published 1897-1904.

SELECTED POEMS

A selection of Noguchi's compressed 'free verse',
published 1896-1909.

NOTES ON HOKKU

A selection of Noguchi's essays & lectures on
hokku & poetics, published 1912-1914.

~~~~~~~~~~~~~~~~~~~~~~~~~~~~~~~~~~~~

BY YONE NOGUCHI

JAPANESE HOKKU

– SELECTED VERSES –

YONE NOGUCHI

1920

Some of these poems are written in measure of seventeen syllables, and the others are more free in forms. But the Japanese Hokku spirit, I believe, runs through all of them.

Hokku means literally a single utterance or the utterance of a single verse; that utterance should be like a " moth light playing on reality's dusk," or " an art hung, as a web, in the air of perfume."

TO
WILLIAM BUTLER YEATS

Suppose the stars
Fall and break?—Do they ever sound
Like my own love song?

The faint shadow of the morning moon?
Nay, the snow falling on the earth.
The mist of blossoming flowers?
Nay, poetry smiling up the sky.

What is life? A voice,
A thought, a light on the dark,—
Lo, crow in the sky.

The seas sleep. The stars—
They are where? Oh my loneliness!
I gaze on my heart.

The far-away sky,
The white billow in distance,
And the expanse of Life and World.

Sudden pain of earth
I hear in the fallen leaf.
"Life's autumn," I cry.

Leaves blown,
Birds flown away.

I wander in and out the Hall of Autumn.

At eve,
By a grass-made hut,
The winds pass on,
Saying something
    to the rice-plant leaves.
I am knocking at the door of Life,—
Is nobody in?

My memory-bird,
To the night's rhythm, soft and sad.
Ghost, art thou not tired?

Lift anchor, life-ship!
Love's red seas, white fancy-birds,
Behold! and the blue.

Are the fallen stars
    Returning up the sky?—
The dews on the grass.

Is it a fallen leaf?
That's my soul sailing on
The silence of Life.

Shadow!
There's shadow!
Heaven's shadow!
  Shadow!
  Shadow!
Of my far-off thought!

Behold the sky where the cuckoo sung,—
There remains the morning moon.

Behold the world where Life cried,—
There remains poetry.

By the path of the breeze,
Love lone but happy sings and roams.

I gather the petals of thought,
Nursed by the slumber of peace.

The voice falls like a dream,
Across the light of forgetfulness.

Eternity rolled in love,
Bids the visible world to sing.

I, a moth with no sense of the day,
Dare not fly,
Lest the silence be marred.

Oh, my own self in the barge
Laden with the memory of mists,
Gliding down by the life-grey stream.

Truth, like moon of day and night,
Ever perfect, all silent and gold,
Shed thy light over sorrow,
Make me regain my rest and song.

A breeze forgotten by life,
Steps from thought to thought.

Oh, peace gained by hushed prayer!

The silence-leaves fallen from Life,
Older than dream or pain,—
Are they my passing ghost?

"Ghost of my soul," I shout,
"That cries only to curse me?"
Tip, tip, tip . . .
        thus the rain falls.

Bits of song . . . what else?
I, a rider of the stream,
Lone between the clouds.

Full of faults, you say.
What beauty in repentance!
Tears, songs . . .
thus life flows

Is it not the cry of a rose to be saved?
Oh, how could I,
When I, in fact, am the rose!

That's the way that the stars grow old,
Is it only that life has to pass away?

Oh, monotonous song that makes me hate myself,
Song of sadness, song of fate!

There's a moment the flower falls into false art,
It's where the poet into mannerism falls too.

It's accident to exist as a flower or a poet:
A mere twist of evolution
          but from the same force.

I see no form but only beauty in evidence:
Oh, imagination and desire,
                    makers of the life and art!

To be the dancer is to make the singer sing.

Is it the pillar by which I reach the sky?
Is it the hill whereon I put my faith?
Is it eternity where songs may find their home?

Crawled? Whereto?
I know nothing except my desire
To hunt after the hidden love,—
A Hamlet across the night and pain.

The ancient song of my heart
Comes and goes in Life's light.

Sudden, a glow, a rainbow,
Draws its line across the breast of my soul.

But the march to Life . . .
Break song to sing the new song!
Clouds leap, flowers bloom.

Song of sea in rain,
Voice of the sky, earth and men!
List, song of my heart,

To become tree-man,
Oh, songs given back by the winds!
What joy of no-man.

Oh, to part now, does it mean that we shall
    meet never again?
To have done forever with joy, thou and I,
Than to begin with pain again!

I shall cry to thee across the years?
Wilt thou turn thy face to respond
To my own tears with thy smile?

The seas are passion-red,
The willows humanity-green.

'Tis thy dream to make the rainbow sing,
To make a stone leap to the sky.

I wish to be like a hurrying, rock-hurling
mountain stream,
Its double torrents by the road of love
will meet in the end.

The voice of the rockets—
Then the flash.

Is it not that of my soul born
    to please the people below,
To take pain of death in her keeping alone?

                To face only the sky and forget the land,
                Oh, to become a rider of the winds!

                What a joy to find a greater
                    song amid the clouds!

Is there anything new under the sun?
Certainly there is.
See how a bird flies, how flowers smile!

I row across the expanse of sea,
And the far-away sky,—
I row across the white billows of pain.

The fickle waves of a strand do drench
my sleeves with sprays:
My songs cry only to make the stars sing.

Let me rise from life's dust,
And save myself from pains.
Who will come with me
    for an hour's carnival?

Where's cherry blossom?
The trace of the garden's breeze is seen no more,
I will point, if I am asked,
To my fancy snow upon the ground.

The snow, like a silent army,
    hurries to the ground;
I, by the fireside, lonely watch the
    yellow hands of flame,
Uplifting as if in prayer.

I look around into the silence of the night.

Creator of attitude and art,
Singer of life's intoxication,
    of youthfulness and revolt.

Oh, spring extravagant and proud!

The wind shook her hair of gloom;
The bleak sun flew down the way
    the sorrow comes forth.
My soul swings
As if a willow leaf.

I turned my face not to see
Flowers or leaves;
'Tis the autumn eve
With the falling light:
How solitary the cottage stands
By the sea!

I sit by a charcoal brazier;
Silence in the wind without calms
    my thought.

I ask myself if the fire is not my own self.
What are the fire-sticks that mock,
    cheat, play with and stir my soul?
Oh, fire-sticks of my imagination,
    handle it kind,
It will soon pass away,
    like the fire, into dust,
        the silence.

The sunlight of morn
Steps into my soul of dream, and says:
"What a wilderness art thou!"

I hide myself behind the biggest billow,—
Oh, what a delight!
How my poor doves search after me!

The nightingales under the boughs,
Sighing now white, now red,
Sing a pearl song
Over the greyness of earth.

Like a cobweb hung upon the tree,
    Prey to wind and sunlight!
Who will say that we are safe and strong?

How sweet is to sleep!
Is there any more sweet word than good-night?

early
HOKKU

YONE NOGUCHI
1897-1904

Since I left California in 1900 for New York and London, I had seen many other cities more big and more prosperous, but my mind always returned to Miller's Heights where my poetry first began to grow amid the roses and carnations which Miller and I watered tenderly.

MAY 5th, 1897: Old man Miller always wears a red silk sash above his pants, even when watering the roses in the garden, and ploughing the fields together. Evening, the moon comes out, and I compose hokku-style poems in English.

昼見れば赤き帶なる螢哉

seen by day
it becomes a red obi . . .
the firefly

[for Joaquin Miller]

Blow out lantern light!
  Walk after the moon along
Love's road into bliss!

Sleep! Silence! And Moon!
    I stand on the mirror-ground
For my night prayer.

The snowy arms push
    The door of my lonely hut?
O Love! My own Moon!

Sun is high, flowers laugh,
    The birds and river sing loud :
And God in my breast.

O song of grayness !
    Lo, the pine upon the hill
Under the blue sky !

The stars sleep ; the sea
    Sleeps in mist : O loneliness !
Boundlessness and I !

O clouds! My sorrow!

    O Moon! O my saddest moon

Of the heart of mine!

Gods of East and West
    Play chess on the sky of night:
" You fool! Stars are they."

O God, how long thou
    Hast to spin the threads of rains
For Spring gown ? Oh, rain !

Shabby home of mine ! Glad
    To have Moon and chrysanthemums,
Three acres of land !

O silent lotus !
    Like a nun it does appear :
Tell me thy sad tale !

The fallen stars there
      Are returning up the skies :
Nay ! fireflies are they.

Under the willow green
Someone stands. It's not my Love,
But the shadow of Moon.

A Proposal to American Poets

FEBRUARY, 1904

HOKKU (seventeen-syllable poem) is like a tiny star, mind you, carrying the whole sky at its back. It is like a slightly-open door, where you may steal into the realm of poesy. It is simply a guiding lamp. Its value depends on how much it suggests. The Hokku poet's chief aim is to impress the reader with the high atmosphere in which they are living. I always compare an English poem with a mansion with windows widely open, even the pictures of its drawing-room being visible from outside. I dare say it does not tempt me much to see the within.

> On a withered branch,
> Lo! the crows are sitting there,
> Oh, this Autumn eve!
> (Basho.)

Pray, you try Japanese Hokku, my American poets! You say far too much, I should say.

Tell me the street to Heaven.
This? Or that? Oh, which?
What webs of streets!

This way? or that way?
Where's the very street to Heaven?
What webs of streets!

Fallen leaves! Nay, spirits?
Shall I go downward with thee
By a stream of fate?

Lo, light and shadow
Journey to the home of night:
Thou and I—to love!

Where the flowers sleep,
Thank God! I shall sleep, to-night.
Oh, Come, butterfly!

My Love's lengthened hair
Swings over me from Heaven's gate :
Lo, Evening's shadow !

Speak not again, Voice!
The silence washes off sins:
Come not again, Light!

Waking or sleeping?
Oh, "No-more" older than world!
Be away, earthly care!

SELECTED POEMS

OF

YONE NOGUCHI

In Memory
of
Basho,
a Hokku Poet
of the
Seventeenth Century

1896 — 1909

Looking back on them now one can see how directly they forecast the modern movement. They were in free verse— in the nineties—they were condensed, suggestive, full of rhythmical variations. In matters of technic they might have been written today, and, though few people understood them then, time has proven Mr. Noguchi a forerunner.

$\left(\text{\textbf{Poetry}} \text{ NOV, 1919}\right)$

Writers of the free verses and the so-called imagists in the present West, let me dare say, will be interested perhaps to know that a Japanese had written such verses like these some twenty four years ago.

$\left(\text{Noguchi Oct. 1920}\right)$

AH, WHO WILL CARE FOR MY POETRY?
I DO NOT KNOW YET BUT I DARE
TO HOPE THAT THERE MAY BE SOME
UNKNOWN FRIENDS AND TO THEM I
LOVINGLY DEDICATE THESE MY SONGS.

*W*HEN I am lost in the deep body of
the mist on the hill,
The world seems built with me as its pillar !
Am I the god upon the face of the deep, deep-
less deepness in the Beginning ?

Seen & Unseen (1896)

I sat alone
In the wood ;
I played music,
I also whistled :
No one knew me
That I was there,
But the moon came
On lover's soft step,
And with the light of Eternity
Suspiciously looked on my mortal soul.

'Sankyo no Nikki' (1897)

Thou, unheard songster—
star with the silent song through the Vast!
O, despair not of to-morrow's dawn !—
those cold mortals forget thy divine beauty.

O, sorrowless home of the twilight,
Where Time is powerless to decay !
There a thousand children
    and mothers play
    surrounding the shadow of God.

Put out the silver lanterns—
the fires of thousand stars !
(Let me sleep !)

Under the hillside boughs,
Oh, this night,
I am beaten by the rain of the cricket song.
(Let me sleep !)

'Sankyo no Nikki' (1897)

The Autumn leaves fall down, fall down,
      Oh, this night,
           Being driven by the wind.
My soul moulders to dust,
      Oh, this night,
           Thinking of my past.
                (Let me sleep!)

'Sankyo no Nikki' (1897)

VI. Puzzling Thought

All the day long
    I watched a stream :
I returned home
    With a puzzling thought.

All the day long
    I wandered amid the wood :
I returned home
    With a puzzling thought.

'Sankyo no Nikki' (1897)

All the day long
    I gazed upon the mountain :
I returned home
    With a puzzling thought.

And in the night
    I stared on the stars :
" Mystery " I said,
    And retired to bed.

'Sankyo no Nikki' (1897)

THE Sierra-rock, a tavern for the
clouds, refuses to let Fame and
Gold sojourn.—
Down the Heaven by the river-road, an
angel's ethereal shadow strays.—
The Genii in the Valley-cavern consult in
silence the message of the Heavens.
O Lord, show unto mortals thy journal —
the balance of Glory and Decay !

The Voice of the Valley (1897)

I HAVE cast the world
And think me as nothing,
Yet I feel cold on snow-falling day,
And happy on flower-day.

SPRING,
Winged Spring,
A laughing butterfly,
Flashes away,
Rosy-cheeked Spring,
Angel of a moment.

THE GODDESS SPINS THE WOOL
OF THE RIVULET TO ITS LENGTH,
O SILVER SONG OF THE FEMALE
  SPINNER !
O GOLDEN SILENCE OF THE
  MALE SPINNER !
GOD IS SPINNING WITH THE
  WHEEL OF TIME; WHITE OF
  DAY AND DARKNESS OF THE
  NIGHT TO ETERNITY.
                    YONE NOGUCHI.

FLORENCE LUNDBORG

From the Eastern Sea (1903)

XI. Life Vessels

THE Life vessels for soul passengers
    glide down the river of Eternity.
O vast river! Solemn river! Yet kind river!
The vessels that are Love-roped by the hand of God
    Sail without failing into the gate of Heaven.

ALAS! my soul is like a paper-lantern,
    its paste wetted off under the rain.

' My love, wilt thou not come back to-night ? '

Lo! the snail at my door stealthily hides his horns.
' Oh, put forth thy honourable horns for my sake !
    Where is Truth ? Where is Light ? '

XII. Lines

OUT of the deep and the dark,
        A sparkling mystery, a shape,
Something perfect,
Comes like the stir of the day :
One whose breath is an odour,
Whose eyes show the road to stars,
The breeze in his face,
The glory of Heaven on his back.
He steps like a vision hung in air,
Diffusing the passion of Eternity ;
His abode is the sunlight of morn,
The music of eve his speech :
In his sight,
One shall turn from the dust of the grave,
And move upward to the woodland.

From the Eastern Sea (1903)

NIGHT! The spirit of resignation homes in the
night. We eloping from the vile land, ask a
lodging of the master of solitude.
O wind! Death-messages from God are sent unto
flowers and leaves. Ah, the autumn with frosting
teeth tells her fate as a deserted wife!
Stillness! All mortals send their dreamships heaven-
ward on the tide of sleep. Thou and I, Charles,
sit alone like two shy stars, west and east.

From the Eastern Sea (1903)

DREAMY Peace dwelt with me, whose magic
vapours enclosed me, softly as lovers' shadows.
 I ever nod upon the graves of Silence.
I ever loll upon waves of muteness, wrapping mists
about my breast.
 I ever roam around the unsettled land of Dawn,
where the ruins moulder into their rest.

IDLY went upward along the stream
 My boat, leaving behind human purpose
 And strife ; lazily went my boat
 Into the indolence, slowly slipping
From the coils of measured distance :
The unhurried course of it was onward.
 My fancies, like living breezes,
  Softly impelled my boat.

XVI. Beyond the Silence [first stanza]

I dreamed I crawled out of darkest hell,
Maddened by the torture of the terrible show,
With blood-shotten eyes numbed by useless gazing
Toward the bliss of the stars.
I crawled out, at last,
Into the breezes of dawn,
Into the breezes whose taste I had forgotten long.
I trembled, feeling the sudden stir of life ;
The green odor of the dawn and immortality
Slowly revived my soul.

Japan of Sword & Love (1905)

XVIII. I Hear You Call, Pine Tree

I hear you call, pine tree, I hear
you upon the hill, by the silent pond
where the lotos flowers bloom, I
hear you call, pine tree.

The Summer Cloud (1906)

What is it you call, pine tree,
when the rains fall, when the winds
blow, and when the stars appear,
what is it you call, pine tree?

I hear you call, pine tree, but I
am blind, and do not know how to
reach you, pine tree. Who will take
me to you, pine tree?

The Summer Cloud (1906)

My little bird, my bird born in my Mother's tears, she flies, stretching her wings so, and from under her wings she drops my Mother's message: "Come home, Beloved!"

Running out from my Mother's bosom, my little river, she suddenly stopped her song, and looking up to the sun, she in her ripples flashed my Mother's message: Beloved, come home!"

The Summer Cloud (1906)

My roses, my little roses grow
in my Mother's breath, they are sad
to-day, casting their faces down;
on their petals I read my Mother's
message: "Come home, beloved!"

The Summer Cloud (1906)

XX. The Dripping Rains

To-day the dripping rains are my comrades.
Their songs are the songs of my soul—
    The songs of love and dreams.
    Where will the rains go?
    Where will my soul go?

The Summer Cloud (1906)

XXI. Spring [excerpts]

In my Lover's eyes brooding upon my soul,

In the song of the skylark,

In my poems,

In the breath of the wind,

In the water-bubbles,

In the lily,

In the tree,

Spring !

The Pilgrimage (1909)

An empty cup whence the light of passion is drunk!—

To-day a sad rumour passes through the trees,

A chill wind is borne by the stream,

The waves shiver in pain ;

Where now the cicada's song long and hot ?

The Pilgrimage (1909)

Here I hear a footstep,

Its voice is grey and soft:

Is it that of a forgotten ghost?

So, a rain-drop drops, ...

Yes, one, two, three.

The Pilgrimage (1909)

Up in the sky there is a cloud,

Its sight is old as Earth :

Who says it is the passing soul ?

At my feet I see a falling leaf,

And the cloud is gone.

After the night wind blows

My soul follows to seek Rest :

Is the wind my mother lost ?

Under the robe of darkness and love

My heart throbs happily with bliss.

The Pilgrimage (1909)

The silence is broken : into the nature
   My soul sails out,
Carrying the song of life on his brow,
   To meet the flowers and birds.

The Pilgrimage (1909)

When my heart returns in the solitude,
  She is very sad,
Looking back on the dead passions
  Lying on Love's ruin.

I am like a leaf
  Hanging over hope and despair,
Which trembles and joins
  The world's imagination and ghost.

The Pilgrimage (1909)

1st Spirit.

Into the leaves the spring of breeze strays,
I, with the bell rung, seek down the road of eve.

2nd Spirit.

The joy of the sea is that of Summer mist,
The rise and fall of tide is my prayer to the heart of song.

The Pilgrimage (1909)

3rd Spirit.

Weaving a dress of journey, I'm Autumn spirit,
My way is where a leaf flies up to the sky.

4th Spirit.

I come down riding on the Winter snow,
Only to wait to be saved by the love of sunlight.

The Pilgrimage (1909)

The mountain green at my right :

The sunlight yellow at my left :

The laughing winds pass between.

The clouds sail away at my right ;

The birds flap down at my left :

The laughing moon appears between.

The Pilgrimage (1909)

I turned left to the dale of poem ;

I turned right to the forest of Love :

But I hurry Home by the road between.

The Pilgrimage (1909)

XXVII. By the Engakuji Temple

Through the breath of perfume,
(O music of musics !)
Down creeps the moon
To fill my cup of song
With memory's wine.

The Pilgrimage (1909)

Across the song of night and moon,
(O perfume of perfumes !)
My soul, as a wind
Whose heart's too full to sing,
Only roams astray   .   .   .

Down the tide of the sweet night
(O the ecstasy's gentle rise !)
The birds, flowers and trees
Are glad at once to fall
Into Oblivion's ruin white.

The Pilgrimage (1909)

XXVIII. At the Yuigahama Shore

Into the homelessness of the sea I awoke :

  Oh, my heart of the wind and spray !

I am glad to be no-man to-day

  With the laughter and dance of the sea-soul.

The Pilgrimage (1909)

Dip the song of the sea and wind,
  Throw it into my heart of longing!
I like to be with the clan of the waters and air:
  Oh, my soul of the sea-soul and surge!

Roll in the wonder of the heart and sea,—
  Oh, my joy of the sea-soul and flash!
Gather all the lights of the wind and sea,
  To guard against the blackest night.

The Pilgrimage (1909)

XXIX. Autumn Song

The gold vision of a bird-wind sways
on the silver foam of song,
The oldest song rises again on
the Autumn heart of dream.

The Pilgrimage (1909)

The ghost castle of glory is built by
the sad magic of Time,
With the last laughter of sorrow,
and with the red tempest
of leaves.

My little soul born out of
the dews of singing dawn,
Bids farewell to the large seas
of Life and speech.

The Pilgrimage (1909)

XXX. The Night Koto Player

The thought of her presence (a bit of flesh and love)
Makes the dusk of night the dusk of perfume.

Sudden as a kiss her rings glow ;
Over the dusk strings her fingers flow as a wave.

The Pilgrimage (1909)

O the breeze of melody of her heart and that of the night,

The ghost musical that dies into the pang of dream !

The Pilgrimage (1909)

Thou burstest from mood :

How sad we have to cling to experience !

Marvel of thy every atom burning in life,

How fully thou livest !

The Pilgrimage (1909)

Didst thou ever think to turn to cold and shadow?

Passionate liver of sunlight,

Symbol of youth and pride ;

Thou art a lyric of thy soaring colour ;

Thy voicelessness of song is action.

What absorption of thy life's meaning,

Wonder of thy consciousness,—

Mighty sense of thy existence !

The Pilgrimage (1909)

Older than love and tears,
Bird of silence born before
the world and wind were made,
Lonely ghost away from laughter and life,
Wing down, I welcome thee,
From the skies of thoughts and stars . . .

With thee, bird of Silence, I long to sail
Beyond the seas where Time and sorrows die,
Bird of silence, dweller of eternity and space,
Make me live in the thought
        before dawn was born . . .

The Pilgrimage (1909)

My song is sung, but a moment . . . .

The song of voice is merely the body,

    (the body dies,)

And the real part of the song, its soul,

    remains after it is sung . . .

The Pilgrimage (1909)

From a Water Color Sketch by M. Takahashi

Yone Noguchi at Home

YONE NOGUCHI, THE POET, AT HIS HOME IN TOKYO

YONE NOGUCHI, THE JAPANESE WRITER, AT WORK.

Thou burstest from mood :
Marvel of thy every atom burning in life,
How fully thou livest !
Passionate lover of sunlight,
Symbol of youth and pride ;
What absorption of thy life's memory,
Wonder of thy consciousness,—
Mighty sense of thy existence !

PORTRAIT OF YONE NOGUCHI, BY O YETO

YONE NOGUCHI

YONÉ NOGUCHI

YONE NOGUCHI

NOTES ON *HOKKU*

excerpts from the essays & lectures of
YONE NOGUCHI

1912-1914

CONTENTS.

From 'A Japanese On English Poetry'
[*The Academy*, Feb. 1912]

I come always to the conclusion... that the English poets waste too much energy in "words, words, and words," and make... their inner meaning frustrate, at least less-distinguished, simply from the reason that its full liberty to appear naked is denied...

I always insist that written poems, even when they are said to be good, are only the second-best, as the very best poems are left unwritten or sung in silence. It is my opinion that the real test for poets is how far they resist their impulse to utterance, or, in another word, to the publication of their own work — not how much they have written, but how much they have destroyed. To live poetry is the main thing, and the question of the poems written or published is indeed secondary; from such a reason I regard our Bashō... as great, while the work credited to his wonderful name could be printed in less than one hundred pages of any ordinary size...

For a poet to have few lines in these prosaic days would be at least an achievement truly heroic; I think that the crusade for Western poetry... as I believe it is most momentous, should begin with the first act of leaving the 'words' behind, or making them return to their original proper places. We have a little homely proverb: "The true heart will be protected by a god, even though it offers no prayer at all." I should like to apply it to poetry and say that poetry will take care of itself, all by itself, without any assistance from words, rhymes, and metres. I flatter myself that even Japan can do something towards the reformation or advancement of Western poetry, not only spiritually, but also physically.

Japanese poetry, at least the old Japanese poetry, is different from Western poetry in the same way as silence is different from a voice, night from day; while avoiding the too close discussion of their relative merits, I can say that the latter always fails... through being too active to properly value inaction, restfulness, or death; to speak shortly, the passive phase of Life and the World. It is fantastic to say that night and day, silence and voice, are all the same; let me admit that they are vastly different; it is their difference that makes them so interesting...

Japanese poetry is that of the moon, stars, and flowers, that of the birds and waterfalls, for the noisiest. If we do not sing so much of Life and the World it is not from the reason that we think their value negative, but from our thought that it would be better, in most cases, to leave them alone, and not to sing of them is the proof of our reverence toward them.

Besides, to sing the stars and the flowers in Japan means to sing Life, since we human beings are not merely a part of Nature, but Nature itself. When our Japanese poetry is best, it is... a searchlight or flash of thought or passion cast on a moment of Life and Nature, which, by virtue of its intensity, leads us to the conception of the whole; it is swift, discontinuous, an isolated piece. So it is that the best of our 17-syllable hokku and 31-syllable uta [tanka] poems, by their art, as Ki no Tsurayuki remarks in his *Kokinshū* preface (c. 905): "Without effort, heaven and earth are moved, and gods and demons invisible to our eyes are touched with sympathy." The real value of Japanese poems may be measured by what mood or illusion they inspire in the reader's mind.

It is not too much to say that an appreciative reader of poetry in Japan is not made, but born, just like a poet; as Japanese poetry is never explanatory, one has everything before them on which to let their imagination freely play; as a result they will come to have an almost personal attachment to it, as much as the author themself. When you realise that the expression or words always mislead you, often making themselves an obstacle to a mood or an illusion, it will be seen what a literary achievement it is when one can say a thing which passes well as real poetry in such a small compass mentioned before; to say "suggestive" is simple enough, the important question is how?

Although I know it sounds rather arbitrary, I may say that such a result may be gained partly (remember, only partly) through determination in the rejection of in-essentials from the phrase and the insistence upon economy of the inner thought; just at this moment, while I write this article, my mind is suddenly recalled to the words which my old California poet-friend used to exclaim: "Cut short, cut short, and again cut short!"

The other day I happened to read the work of Miss Lizette Woodworth Reese, whose sensitiveness... expressed in language of pearl-like simplicity... makes me think of her as a Japanese poet among Americans... As a specimen let me give you the following;

Oh, gray and tender is the rain,
That drips, drips on the pane;
A hundred things come in at the door,
The scent of herbs, the thought of yore.

I see the pool out in the grass,
A bit of broken glass;
The red flags running wet and straight,
Down to the little flapping gate.

Lombardy poplars tall and three,
Across the road I see.
There is no loveliness so plain,
As a tall poplar in the rain.

But oh, the hundred things and more
That come in at the door;
The smack of mint, old joy, old pain,
Caught in the gray and tender rain.

With all due respect, I thought afterwards what a pity to become an American poet if she has to begin her poem with "Oh, gray and tender is the rain" — such a commonplace beginning. I declare bluntly that I, "as a Japanese poet," would sacrifice the first three stanzas to make the last sparkle fully and unique like a perfect diamond... Although it is said that her rejection of inessentials is the secret to her personality and style, it seems that this rejection is not sufficient for my Japanese mind... True poetry should be written only to one's own heart to record the pain or joy, like a soul's diary whose sweetness can be kept when it is hidden secretly, or like a real prayer for which only a few words uttered with blood is enough.

<u>From 'Hokku'</u>
[*The Academy*, July 1912]

The word 'epigram' is no right word (and there's no right word at all) for 'hokku', the 17-syllable poem of Japan... If I rightly understand the word 'epigram', it is or at least looks to have one object... of practical use, to express something... decorative at best...

What our hokku aims at is, a usefulness of uselessness, not what it expresses but how it expresses itself spiritually; its real value is not in its physical directness but in its psychological indirectness. To use a simile, it is like a dew upon lotus leaves of green, or under maple leaves of red, which, although it is nothing but a trifling drop of water, shines, glitters, and sparkles now pearl-white, then amethyst-blue, again ruby-red, according to the time of day and situation.

Better still to say, this hokku is like a spider-thread laden with the white summer dews, swaying among the branches of a tree like an often invisible ghost in [the] air, on the perfect balance; that sway indeed, not the thread itself, is the beauty of our 17-syllable poem.

From 'What Is A Hokku Poem?'
[*Rhythm*, Jan. 1913]

To call the hokku poem suggestive is almost wrong, although it has become a recent fashion for Western critics to interpret, not only... hokku but all Japanese poetry (even my work included), by that one word, because the hokku poem itself is distinctly clear-cut like a diamond or star, never mystified by any cloud or mist like Truth or Beauty...

It is all very well if you have a suggestive attitude of mind in reading it... and I am willing to endorse you when you say the hokku poem is suggestive in the same sense that 'truth' and 'humanity' are suggestive. But I can say myself as a poet (am I too bold to claim that word?) that your poem would certainly end in artificiality if you start out to be suggestive from the beginning; I value the hokku poem, at least some of them, because of its own truth and humanity simple and plain...

I always thought that the most beautiful flowers grow close to the ground, and they need no hundred petals for expressing their own beauty; how can you call it real poetry if you cannot tell it by a few words? Therefore these 17-syllables are just enough, at least to our Japanese mind. And if you cannot express all by one hokku, then you can say it in many hokku; yes, that is all...

I confess that I secretly desired to become a hokku poet in my younger days, that is now 20 years ago, and I used to put the hokku collections of Bashō or Buson with Spencer's Education in the same drawer of my desk... I did not forget to carry with me the hokku collection of Bashō or Buson or some other poet in my American life, even when I did the so-called 'tramp life' in 1895-1898 through the California fields full of buttercups, by the mountain where the cypress trees beckoned my soul to fly, not merely because the thought of home and longing for it was then my only comfort, but more because by the blessing of the book – I mean the *hokku* book – I entered straight into the great heart of Nature. When I left the Pacific Slope in later years towards the Eastern cities built by 'modern' civilisation and machineries, I suddenly thought I had lost the secret understanding of the hokku poems born in Japan, insignificant like a lakeside reed and irresponsible like a dragon-fly; how could you properly understand, for instance, the following hokku poem in [a] New York of skyscrapers and automobiles;

A cloud of flowers!
Is the bell from Ueno
Or Asakusa?

[Bashō, 1644-1694]

Although I was quite loyal to this 17-syllable form of Japanese poetry during many years of my foreign wandering, [since moving to England] I had scarcely any moment to write a hokku in original Japanese or English, till the day when I most abruptly awoke in 1902 to the noise of Charing Cross where I wrote as follows;

Tell me the streets to Heaven
This? Or that? Oh, which?
What webs of streets!

In September 1904, I returned home; the tender silken autumnal rain that was Japanese poetry, and my elder brother, welcomed me (what a ghost, tired and pale I was then), and I was taken to his house in the Nihonbashi district of Tōkyō to wash off my foreign dust and slowly renew my old acquaintance with things Japanese...

From 'Japanese Poetry'
[The Spirit of Japanese Poetry, 1914]

We treat poetry, though it may sound too ambitious to the Western mind, from the point of its use of uselessness; it rises, through a mysterious way, to the height of its peculiar worth, where its uselessness turns, lo, to usefulness. When one knows that the things useless are the things most useful under different circumstances – to give one example, a little stone lazy by a stream, which becomes important when you happen to hear its sermon – one will see that the aspect of uselessness in poetry is to be doubly valued since its usefulness is always born from it like the day out of the bosom of night...

I know that at least in Japan the best poetry was produced in [an] age when publication was most difficult; I dare say that the modern opening of the pages for poets in the press, and the easy publication of their work in independent books, both in the West and the East, would never be the right way for the real encouragement of poetry. I read somewhere that a certain distinguished European actress declared that the true salvation of the stage should start with the destruction of all the theaters in existence; I should like to say... the same thing in regard to the real revival of poetry.

Let the poets forget for once and all about publication, and let them live in poetry as the true poets of old days used to live. Indeed, to live in poetry is first and last. When one talks on the union of poetry and life, I am sure that so it should be in action and practice, not only in print. I have seen so many poets who only live between the covers and die when the ink fades away... Let me learn of death to truly live; let me be silent to truly sing.

From 'The Japanese Hokku Poem'
[*The Spirit of Japanese Poetry*, 1914]

I.

Walter Pater, in one of his much-admired studies, *The School of Giorgione*, represents art as continually struggling after the law or principle of music, toward a condition which music alone completely realises; "lyrical poetry," he thinks, "approaches nearest to that condition, hence is the highest and most complete form of poetry; and," he adds, "the very perfection of such poetry often appears to depend, in part, on a certain suppression or vagueness of mere subjects, so that the meaning reaches us through ways not distinctly traceable by the understanding . . ."

> Oh, how cool—
> The sound of the bell that leaves
> The bell itself.
>
> [Buson, 1716-1784]

I should like to develop Pater's literary ideal a little further through Lao Tze's canon of spiritual anarchism (it's nothing so strange to speak sometimes the names of ancient Chinese sages and modern English critics side by side): is it not that to mean nothing means all things? Again, not to sing at all means to sing everything? Lao Tze says: "Assert non-assertion. Practice non-practice. Taste non-taste." Let me here add one more line: "Express in non-expression." To attach too closely to the subject matter in literary expression is never a way to complete the real saturation; the real infinite significance will only be accomplished at such a consummate moment when the end and means are least noticeable, and the subject and expression never fluctuate from each other, being in perfect collocation; it is the partial loss of the birthright of each that gains an artistic triumph.

I have a word which is much used carelessly in the West, but whose true meaning is only seldom understood, that is the word of *suggestion*. I have an art; that is the art of suggestion. What suggestion, you might ask? I will point the way, if you are given a right sort of artistic susceptibility, where the sunlight falls on the laughter of woods and waters, where the birds sing by the flowers; again I will point if you are able to read the space between the lines, to the pages of the Japanese 17-syllable hokku poems, the tiniest poems of the world.

> The night of spring,—
> Oh, between the eve
> And the dawn.
>
> [Buson, 1716-1784]

I don't mean that the hokku poems are lyrical poetry in the general Western understanding; but [in hokku]... the mind gets the effect before perceiving the fact of their brevity, its sensibility resounding to their single note, as if the calm bosom of river water to the song of a bird... I do not see why we cannot call them musical when we call the single note of a bird musical; indeed, they attain to a condition, as Pater remarked, which music alone completely realises, because what they aim at and practice is the evocation of mood or psychological intensity, not the physical explanation... And even from the narrow scientific understanding of the term they are musical, as they are the first 17-syllables out of the euphonic 31-syllable uta poem, whose birth, according to the mythological assumption, was in the same time when heaven and earth were created...

II.

Lying ill on a journey,
Ah, my dreams run about
The ruin of fields.

[Bashō, 1644-1694]

The above poem of Bashō's recalls to my mind
Walt Whitman's pathos of his last years;

I am an open air man: winged.
I am an open water man: aquatic.
I want to get out, fly, swim—
I am eager for feet again.
But my feet are eternally gone.

[Whitman, 1819-1892]

I read somewhere of Whitman denying the so-
called "literature" (accidentally laughing, scorning, jeering
at his contemporaries): "I feel about literature what
Grant did about war. He hated war. I hate literature. I
am not a literary West Pointer, I do not love a literary
man as a literary man, as a minister of a pulpit loves
other ministers, because they are ministers. It is a means
to an end, that is all there is to it: I never attribute
any other significance to it."

Bashō always spoke from the same reason
that there was no other poetry except the poetry of
the heart; he never thought literature or so-called literature
to be connected with his own poetry, because it was
a single noted adoration or exclamation offhand at
the almost dangerous moment when his love of
Nature suddenly turned to hatred from the too great excess
of his love. It is the word of exclamation; its brevity
is strength of his love. Hokku means literally a single

utterance or the utterance of a single verse: that utterance should be like a "moth light playing on reality's dusk," or "an art hung, as a web, in the air of perfume," swinging soft in [the] music of a moment.

Now again to return to Whitman. He remarks somewhere: "New York gives the literary man a touch of sorrow; he is never quite the same human being after New York has really set in; the best fellows have few chances of escape." Although Bashō never expressed his hatred of city life in such a bold emphasis of words as Whitman... the fact of his spending the greater part of his life, now on the sleepy back of a horse by a whispering stream, then seeing the fallen petals in deep sigh with country rustics, is proof enough that he regarded city life as fatal to his poetry. He was, with Whitman, a good exemplar to teach us how to escape the burden of life; and again, hokku poems, if intelligently translated into English (indeed that is an almost impossible literary feat to accomplish), will give the most interesting example to encourage the modern literary ideal of the West, which seeks its salvation in escape from the so-called 'literary'.

When I say the best hokku poems 'do not know their own limitations' (remember, they are only 17-syllables), that is because they are of the most essential of all the essential languages, which is inwardly extensive and outwardly vague; a severe restraint imposed on one side will be well balanced by the large freedom on the other. As in any poem of any other country, the Japanese poet's work also rests on the belief that poetry should express 'truth' in its own way; by that truth we Japanese mean Nature; again by that Nature the order of *spontaneity*.

Lao Tze says: "People takes their law from the Earth; the Earth its law from Heaven; Heaven its law from Tao; but the law of Tao in its own spontaneity." It was the Chinese sage's greatness to interpret... psychologically

'God' by the single word of spontaneity. When I measure our Japanese poetical truth by the said spontaneity, my mind dwells on the best hokku poems as the songs "with no words, not tyrannised by form."

They are the voice of spontaneity which makes an unexpected assault upon Poetry's summit; the best expression for it would be, of course, 'suggestion', or [a] hint of its eccentricity or emphasis. As the so-called 'literary' expression is a secondary matter in the realm of poetry, there is no strict boundary between the domains [that are] generally called subjective and objective. While some hokku poems appear to be 'objective', those poems are again by turns quite 'subjective', through the great virtue of the writers having the fullest identification with the matter written on.

You might call such collation poetical trespassing; but it is the very point whence the Japanese poetry gains unusual freedom; that freedom makes us join at once with the soul of Nature. I admit that when such poetical method is carried to the extreme, there will result unintelligibility; but poetical unintelligibility is certainly better than the imbecility or vulgarity of which examples abound, permit me to say, in English poetry. It is the aim of this Japanese poetry that each line of the poem should appeal to the reader's consciousness, perhaps with the un-connected words, touching and again kindling on the particular association; there is ample reason to say that our poetry is really searching for a far more elusive effect than the general English poetry.

As I said before, the hokku poems are, unlike the majority of English poems, the expression of the moods or forces of the writer's poetical exertion, and their aim, if aim they have, is hardly connected with the thing or matter actually stated, but it casts a light on the poetical position in which the writer stands. Although the phrase might be taken wrongly in the West, our Japanese poets at their best, as in the case of some of William Blake's work, are the poets of attitude who depend so much on the intelligent sympathy of their readers. Their work is like a silent bell of a Buddhist temple; it may not mean anything for some people, like that bell which has no voice at all. But the bell rings out, list, in a golden voice, when there is a person who strikes it; and what voice the bell should have will depend on the other.

[The Keys/Of the Gates]
The caterpillar on the leaf
Reminds thee of thy mother's grief.
[Blake, 1757-1827]

And again the hokku poem is a bell helpless, silent, [with no] reader to cooperate. When I say that the readers of Japanese poetry, particularly hokku poems, should be born like a poet, I count, I should say, their personal interest almost as much as that of the writers themselves. Therefore in our poetry the readers assume an equally responsible place; and they can become, if they like, creators of poems which in fact are not their own work, just as if one with a bell-hammer did create the bell in the real sense.

III.

I have quite an interest in the pages of English translation or free rendering of our Japanese poetry, because I learn from them the point of the Western choice of the subjects, and where the strength or weakness of the English mind lies in poetical writing. Take the following hokku poem, [by Chiyo];

Asagao ni
Tsurube torarete
Morai mizu
[Chiyo, 1703-1775]

With the translation by Edwin Arnold;

The morning-glory
Her leaves and bells has bound
My bucket handle round.
I could not break the bands
Of these soft hands.
The bucket and the well to her left,
"Let me some water, for I come bereft."
[tr. Arnold, c. 1897]

And Miss Clara Walsh;

All round the rope a morning glory clings;
How can I break its beauty's dainty spell
I beg for water from a neighbor's well.
[tr. Walsh, 1910]

With due respect to these translators, I ask myself why the English mind must spend so much ink while we Japanese are well satisfied with the following;

The well-bucket taken away
By the morning-glory—
Alas, water to beg!
[tr. Noguchi]

Is it not the exact case as when the Western fountain-pen attempts to copy a Japanese picture drawn with bamboo brush and incensed Indian ink on a rice paper, in which formlessness, like that of a summer

cloud, is often a passport into the sky of a higher art...
When the English poet must cling to such an exactitude,
let me dare say, as if a tired swimmer with a life-belt, I
have only to wonder at the general difference between
East and West in the matter of poetry. Take another
example to show in what direction the English poetical
mind pleases to turn [at the time, often quoted by English
and American translators];

> I thought I saw the fallen leaves
> Returning to their branches:
> Alas, butterflies were they.
>
> [Moritake, 1473-1549]

What real poetry is in the above, I wonder, except
a pretty, certainly not high ordered, fancy of a vignettist;
it might pass as a fitting specimen if we understand
hokku poems, as some Western students delight to
understand hokku poems, by the word 'epigram'. Although
my understanding of that word is not necessarily limited
to the thought of a pointed saying, I may not be
much mistaken to compare the word with a still, almost
dead pond where thought or fancy, nay the water, hardly
changes or procreates itself; hokku, at least in my mind,
are a running living water of poetry where you can
reflect yourself to find your own identification (therefore
the best hokku poem is least translatable in English, or
perhaps in any language).

It is, as I wrote already somewhere, "like a
dew upon lotus leaves of green, or under maple-leaves
of red, which, though it is nothing but a trifling drop
of water, shines, glitters, and sparkles now pearl-white,
then amethyst-blue, again ruby-red, according to the
time of day and situation; better still to say this hokku
is like a spider-thread laden with the white summer
dews, swaying among the branches of a tree like

an often invisible ghost in the air, on the perfect balance; that sway indeed, not the thread itself, is the beauty of our 17-syllable poem."

But you must know that such language can only apply to the very best hokku, which, when introduced with sympathy rather than mere intelligence, will serve – through their magic of 'potential speech', to use Arthur Ransome's phrase, or, let me say, 'potential effect' – the modern Western writers or poets, as I said before, in search of an escape from the so-called literature. And these very best hokku poems cannot be, in my opinion, more than half a thousand, nay, perhaps not more than two hundred and fifty in number from all works written in the last three hundred years. As there are indeed a most prodigious number of productions, my estimate will show, I believe, that even a dozen good hokku in one's whole life would not be regarded as a bad crop.

In fact, the hokku poems produced in the time before great Bashō's (1644-1694) appearance, when, under the influence of Teitoku (1570-1653), Teishitsu (1610-1673), and Sōin (1605-1682) – the school of art for art's sake, from the point of intricacy, mannerism, and affectation – are certainly not better than the butterfly poem quoted above.

> Alas, lonesome road,
> Deserted by wayfarers,
> This autumn evening!
> [Bashō, 1644-1694]

[And] although Bashō and his disciples (it is said that Bashō had three thousand disciples or followers in his life's days) rescued poetry from the hands of such a school of artistic vulgarity, the Shōfu which he established... became soon again sadly degenerated; and it was Buson (1716-84) who... cried out for the so-called poetical revival of the Tenmei period. There was no more popular poetry once than this hokku form, and it is still popular even today, when our insularity, poetical or otherwise, has been irrevocably broken.

It goes without saying that wherever there was a great master, there was a great hokku poem: which never makes us notice its limitation of form, but rather impresses us by the freedom through mystery of its chosen language, as if a sea-crossing wind blown in from a little window. There have been, since the Grand Restoration, a few bold attempts at a hokku revival, notably that of the late Shiki (1867-1902); but it is not my present aim to follow after their historical record. What I hope to do at this moment is to point out to you the very value of the Japanese poetry of this peculiar form.

It's light—
The snow upon my hat,
When it's mine.

[Kikaku, 1661-1707]

Arthur Ransome says somewhere in his paper called 'Kinetic and Potential Speech': "It is like a butterfly that has visited flowers and scatters their scent in its flight. The scent and the fluttering of its bloom-laden wings are more important than the direction or speed of its flying." Such language applies to the hokku poems at their best. I agree with Ransome in saying: "Poetry is made by a combination of kinetic with potential speech. Eliminate either, and the result is no longer poetry." But you must know that the part of kinetic speech is left quite unwritten in the hokku poem, and that the kinetic language in your mind should combine its force with the potential speech of the poem itself, and make the whole thing at once complete. Indeed, it is the readers who make the hokku's imperfection a perfection of art.

*More Thought
Space*

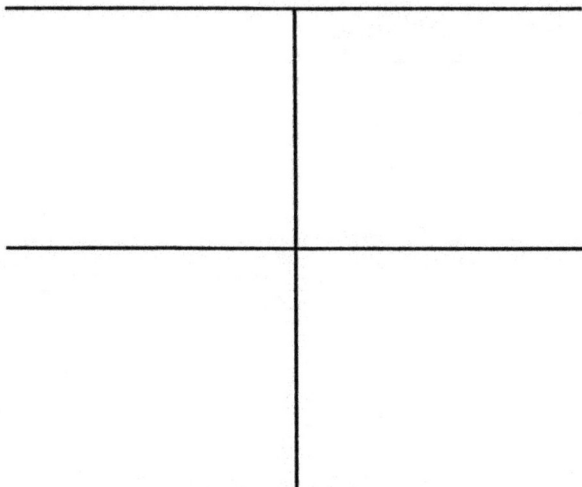

Please handle with care.

www.ingramcontent.com/pod-product-compliance
Lightning Source LLC
La Vergne TN
LVHW041321080426
835513LV00008B/536